D1050395

LIFE IS TOO SHORT . . .

Life is too short...

Helen Bland, Patti Falzarano,
Bo Niles, and Mary Sears

WARNER BOOKS

A Time Warner Company

Warner Books, Inc., 1271 Avenue of the Americas, New York, NY 10020

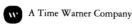 A Time Warner Company

Printed in the United States of America
First Printing: January 1994
10 9 8 7 6 5 4 3 2

Library of Congress Cataloging-in-Publication Data
Life is too short— / Helen Bland . . . [et al.].
    p.   cm.
  ISBN 0-446-39523-4
  1. Life—Humor.   2. American wit and humor.   I. Bland, Helen
  Baine.
PN6231.L48L54   1994
818' .540208—dc20

93—10160
CIP

Book design by H. Roberts
Cover illustration by Merle Nacht
Cover design by Julia Kushnirsky

INTRODUCTION

"Life is short. Eat dessert first."

These few words, simple but rife with philosophical significance, inspired us to write this book.

As we pondered their meaning one day, we decided it was high time to look at our own baggage, to see what we could purposely toss off the train to make the trip through life more enjoyable.

Our first thought was "Life is too short to miss writing a book together." Then we got down to business.

Here are a few "unessentials" we'll gladly jettison, and some "essentials" we'll *never* give up!

Life Is Too Short . . .

❑ to watch reruns
❑ to procrastinate
❑ to worry about appearances
❑ to have twenty-twenty hindsight
❑ to believe everything you read

LIFE IS TOO SHORT . . .

- ❏ to stuff a mushroom
- ❏ to devein shrimp
- ❏ to shave a peach
- ❏ to peel a grape
- ❏ to eat winter tomatoes

Life Is Too Short . . .

❏ to count to ten without screaming
❏ to blend your makeup with a sponge
❏ to move the piano
❏ to rake the carpet
❏ to sell your house yourself

LIFE IS TOO SHORT . . .

Not to:

- ❏ lie in a hammock
- ❏ wear a helmet
- ❏ start a nest egg
- ❏ pop the question
- ❏ create your own traditions

4

LIFE IS TOO SHORT . . .

Not to:

- ❏ be a kid as long as you can
- ❏ speak your mind
- ❏ giggle with your children
- ❏ ignore the alarm clock now and then
- ❏ ride the pony at the grocery store

LIFE IS TOO SHORT . . .

❏ to break your fingernails on complicated
  packaging
❏ to answer nosy questions
❏ to suck the filling out of a Twinkie
❏ to have dressing on the side
❏ to warm the dinner plates

Life Is Too Short . . .

- ❑ to act superior
- ❑ to be a martyr
- ❑ to turn a deaf ear
- ❑ to harass anyone
- ❑ to wait for him–or her–to call

LIFE IS TOO SHORT . . .

Not to:

- ❑ soak up the latest gossip
- ❑ chase a rainbow
- ❑ lick the Oreo filling first
- ❑ gambol and cavort on the first day of spring
- ❑ get involved

8

LIFE IS TOO SHORT . . .

Not to:

- ❏ shoot the rapids
- ❏ hold hands
- ❏ choose a good wine
- ❏ drop everything and go fishing
- ❏ nap on a lazy Saturday

Life Is Too Short . . .

❏ to read between the lines
❏ to stand on line
❏ to be handed a line

LIFE IS TOO SHORT . . .

❑ to remember the seven deadly sins
the eight wonders of the
world
the five food groups
the seven dwarfs
the eight reindeer

LIFE IS TOO SHORT . . .

Not to:

- ❑ strike up the band
- ❑ strike it rich
- ❑ strike out on your own

LIFE IS TOO SHORT . . .

Not to:
- ❏ catch a fly
- ❏ fly a kite
- ❏ fly first class

LIFE IS TOO SHORT . . .

❏ to sit in the middle
❏ to let the snow stop you
❏ to let your weight stop you
❏ to swim upstream
❏ to put up with the previous owners' carpeting

LIFE IS TOO SHORT . . .

❏ to deadhead rhodies
❏ to make a gingerbread house
❏ to check your luggage
❏ to go to someone else's school recital
❏ to worry about hem lengths

LIFE IS TOO SHORT . . .

Not to:

- ❑ give an ump the raspberry
- ❑ zip up
- ❑ hug yourself
- ❑ travel light

LIFE IS TOO SHORT . . .

Not to:

- ❏ go for the gold
- ❏ look for the silver lining
- ❏ catch the brass ring

LIFE IS TOO SHORT . . .

❑ to tease your hair (or any other animal)
❑ to talk to a computer on the phone
❑ to worry about how many angels fit on the
   head of a pin
❑ to needle your little brother
❑ to learn how to program the VCR

Life Is Too Short . . .

❑ to answer a phone survey
❑ to argue heredity versus environment
❑ to make hollandaise
❑ to throw in the towel
❑ to mend anything

LIFE IS TOO SHORT . . .

Not to:

- ❏ thumb your nose
- ❏ do the wave
- ❏ go camping
- ❏ catch a sunrise
- ❏ learn the hula or the mambo

20

LIFE IS TOO SHORT . . .

Not to:

- ❏ fall in love
- ❏ give 'em hell
- ❏ get down and dirty
- ❏ rent a red convertible
- ❏ wear leopard spike heels to a Republican rally

LIFE IS TOO SHORT . . .

❏ to field a question
❏ to make your own paper
❏ to match black velvets
❏ to exercise for fun
❏ to act your age

22

LIFE IS TOO SHORT . . .

❏ to de-thatch the lawn
❏ to play it safe
❏ to knot your own bow tie
❏ to make an elephant topiary
❏ to grin and bear it

23

LIFE IS TOO SHORT . . .

Not to:

☐ buy the next size up
☐ ride a roller coaster
☐ make hay while the sun shines
☐ march in a Fourth of July parade

24

LIFE IS TOO SHORT . . .

Not to:
- ❏ be a princess
- ❏ be queen for a day
- ❏ duke it out with the bad guys
- ❏ appoint yourself king

25

LIFE IS TOO SHORT . . .

❑ to say *yes* when you want to say *no* to
>   a party
>   a covered-dish supper
>   taking someone else's turn at
>   car pool

LIFE IS TOO SHORT . . .

❏ to say *no* when you want to say *yes* to
> a candy bar
> the last bite of a shared dessert
> a flirtatious glance

LIFE IS TOO SHORT . . .

Not to:

❏ kiss and make up

❏ wear a costume on Halloween

❏ order à la carte

❏ have a tea party with your daughter

❏ search for the sublime

Life Is Too Short . . .

Not to:
- ❏ share fishing secrets
- ❏ jump in a pile of leaves
- ❏ wear your headband
- ❏ exhibit grace under pressure
- ❏ have a confidante

LIFE IS TOO SHORT . . .

❑ to look up a number in the phone book
❑ to try to figure people out
❑ to save old clothes for the future
❑ to wait on hold listening to Muzak
❑ to measure your body fat

LIFE IS TOO SHORT . . .

❑ to fold napkins into swans
❑ to make radish roses
❑ to steam off a stamp
❑ to give up ice cream
❑ to remember you forgot

Life Is Too Short . . .

Not to:

- ❏ toast marshmallows
- ❏ toast your friends
- ❏ toast your ancestors

Life Is Too Short . . .

Not to:
- ❏ laugh at yourself
- ❏ stand by your mate
- ❏ head for the coast
- ❏ tie your own flies
- ❏ meet someone halfway

Life Is Too Short . . .

❏ to diagram a sentence
❏ to blot your lipstick
❏ to do Barbie's hair
❏ to pretend you're something you're not
❏ to work on your day off

LIFE IS TOO SHORT . . .

❏ to groom your own dog
❏ to make your own costume
❏ to know your spouse completely
❏ to dot every *i* and cross every *t*
❏ to argue with your kids about what they're
going to wear

35

LIFE IS TOO SHORT . . .

Not to:

- ❏ use your best china
- ❏ take the bull by the horns
- ❏ store snowballs in the freezer
- ❏ take a stand
- ❏ count your blessings

36

LIFE IS TOO SHORT . . .

Not to:

- ❑ cross party lines
- ❑ drink fresh-squeezed orange juice
- ❑ wade in a cold mountain stream
- ❑ see the northern lights
- ❑ throw confetti

LIFE IS TOO SHORT . . .

❏ to buy green bananas
❏ to sort socks
❏ to convert inches to centimeters
❏ to watch the news at six *and* eleven
❏ to fake it

LIFE IS TOO SHORT . . .

❏ to do things you're not good at
❏ to corral dust bunnies
❏ to trust the weather report
❏ to wear panty hose in the summer
❏ to burn your bridges

LIFE IS TOO SHORT . . .

- ❑ to send a chain letter
- ❑ to spell your name every time
- ❑ to bear a grudge
- ❑ to find the missing puzzle piece

LIFE IS TOO SHORT . . .

❏ to be a square
❏ to square off
❏ to go back to square one

41

LIFE IS TOO SHORT . . .

Not to:

- ❏ play catch with your kids
- ❏ have a favorite chair
- ❏ use the drive-through window
- ❏ wear cashmere
- ❏ wait your turn

42

LIFE IS TOO SHORT . . .

Not to:
- ❏ bake a cake from scratch
- ❏ climb a mountain
- ❏ go to the family reunion
- ❏ mark the door frame as they grow
- ❏ make a wish list

43

LIFE IS TOO SHORT . . .

❑ to disagree with your cat about property
rights
❑ to make much ado about nothing
❑ to play second fiddle
❑ to quibble

44

LIFE IS TOO SHORT . . .

❑ to make excuses
❑ to be petty
❑ to throw your weight around
❑ to keep something because you never know
  when it will come in handy
❑ to Monday-morning quarterback

LIFE IS TOO SHORT . . .

❏ to run around
❏ to run aground
❏ to run amok

LIFE IS TOO SHORT . . .

❏ to figure out the pH of your skin
                            your hair
                            the soil

LIFE IS TOO SHORT . . .

Not to:

- ☐ make Thanksgiving dinner
- ☐ take a mental health day
- ☐ make up your own mind
- ☐ buy "those" shoes
- ☐ take a chance

Life Is Too Short . . .

Not to:

- ❏ let yourself go
- ❏ watch a porpoise play
- ❏ be someone's cheerleader
- ❏ make snow angels
- ❏ watch Ed Sullivan again

LIFE IS TOO SHORT . . .

❏ to suck in your gut
❏ to shoot off your mouth
❏ to keep a stiff upper lip

LIFE IS TOO SHORT . . .

❏ to be a snake in the grass
❏ to fish for compliments
❏ to look a gift horse in the mouth

LIFE IS TOO SHORT . . .

❑ to fight with cling wrap
❑ to stay under budget
❑ to cuff trousers
❑ to dust the top of the refrigerator
❑ to make a scene

LIFE IS TOO SHORT . . .

❏ to attack, assault, or assail
❏ to beset, besiege, or beleaguer
❏ to sulk, pout, or scowl
❏ to pull strings or pull rank
❏ to beg to differ

LIFE IS TOO SHORT . . .

Not to:

- ❑ look for Elvis
- ❑ listen to your parents
- ❑ grow a beard
- ❑ help a turtle across the street
- ❑ wear your heart on your sleeve

LIFE IS TOO SHORT . . .

Not to:

- ❏ use Velcro
- ❏ say hi
- ❏ say please
- ❏ chase lightning bugs
- ❏ recycle

LIFE IS TOO SHORT . . .

❑ to pass the buck
❑ to listen to a lounge lizard
❑ to watch infomercials
❑ to read yesterday's news
❑ to skip anything because your horoscope
  says to

LIFE IS TOO SHORT . . .

❏ to wash the cat
❏ to bury the guppie
❏ to brush the dog's teeth
❏ to cut your rabbit's toenails
❏ to teach a pig to sing

LIFE IS TOO SHORT . . .

❏ to have a chatty dentist
❏ to use hair spray
❏ to get stuck with a boor
❏ to miss an eclipse
❏ to put up with bad manners

Life Is Too Short . . .

❏ to figure out a magic trick
❏ to open mail addressed to "occupant"
❏ to laugh up your sleeve
❏ to cut with a dull knife
❏ to settle for anything

LIFE IS TOO SHORT . . .

Not to:

- ❏ slow dance
- ❏ take a long hot shower
- ❏ plant a seedling
- ❏ share your lunch
- ❏ dream in color

LIFE IS TOO SHORT . . .

Not to:

❑ go the distance
❑ clap for Tinkerbell
❑ scream for your team
❑ cry at the sad parts
❑ laugh until you cry

LIFE IS TOO SHORT . . .

❑ to presoak
    hold and rinse
    hand wash
    dry flat

LIFE IS TOO SHORT . . .

❑ to turn up your nose
        down a bed
        away a friend
        back the clock

Life Is Too Short . . .

❏ to mold gelatin
❏ to sing "Ninety-nine Bottles of Beer on the Wall"
❏ to have a "hairdo"
❏ to eat chocolate-covered ants
❏ to count your change before leaving the toll booth

LIFE IS TOO SHORT . . .

❑ to fight over the remote control
         the toothpaste tube
         who left the lights on
         who left the cage open
         a parking space

LIFE IS TOO SHORT . . .

❏ to sling mud
❏ to miss the exit
❏ to throw a game
❏ to break a promise
❏ to set a timetable

LIFE IS TOO SHORT . . .

❏ to master bridge
>>> port and starboard
>>> effect and affect
>>> crossword puzzle-ese
>>> your computer instruction
>>> manual

Life Is Too Short . . .

Not to:

- ❏ bring your pillow on vacation
- ❏ pull out those first gray hairs
- ❏ run through a fountain
- ❏ do the crossword in ink
- ❏ learn an instrument

LIFE IS TOO SHORT . . .

Not to:

- ❏ boo when the Grinch steals Christmas
- ❏ cheer when he brings it back
- ❏ visit the White House
- ❏ tell the dentist when it hurts
- ❏ blow your own horn

LIFE IS TOO SHORT . . .

❑ to marry an early bird
❑ to bitch and moan
❑ to dwell on "what-ifs"
❑ to take yourself seriously
❑ to drone on

LIFE IS TOO SHORT . . .

❑ to give up chocolate
❑ to sort through dried beans
❑ to make individual pizzas
❑ to serve "designer" water
❑ to carve ice sculptures

Life Is Too Short . . .

❏ to count stitches

       sheep

       your chickens before they hatch

       sheets of competing brands of
           toilet tissue

       someone else's items in the express
           line

LIFE IS TOO SHORT . . .

❏ to stretch a dollar
        a meal
        last year's spandex swimsuit

Life Is Too Short . . .

❏ to follow the herd
❏ to blame your parents
❏ to excavate a turkey carcass for leftovers
❏ to paint a ceiling
❏ to match gravel pebbles

74

LIFE IS TOO SHORT . . .

❏ to forget your PIN number
❏ to balance your checkbook
❏ to pinch a penny
❏ to trade in futures
❏ to be penny-wise and pound-foolish

LIFE IS TOO SHORT . . .

Not to:

❑ stop at a tag sale

❑ stop at an outlet store

❑ stop on a dime

LIFE IS TOO SHORT . . .

Not to:
- ❏ fingerpaint
- ❏ paint your wagon
- ❏ paint the town red

LIFE IS TOO SHORT . . .

❏ to shave on vacation
❏ to learn quantum physics
❏ to get sprayed by a perfume demonstrator
❏ to rue the day
❏ to keep up with the Joneses

Life Is Too Short . . .

❏ to suffer starched collars—or stuffed shirts
❏ to do a single-color jigsaw puzzle
❏ to be a nitpicker
❏ to inject individual strawberries with
   liqueur
❏ to boast

LIFE IS TOO SHORT . . .

Not to:

- ❏ overtip
- ❏ eat Chinese food out of the container
- ❏ wish upon a star
- ❏ sing along
- ❏ care

Life Is Too Short . . .

Not to:

- ❏ bury the hatchet
- ❏ dine by candlelight
- ❏ talk to the animals
- ❏ buy that great car
- ❏ plunge down a water slide

LIFE IS TOO SHORT . . .

Not to:

- ❏ skip a stone
- ❏ twist and shout
- ❏ jump rope
- ❏ soar in a hot-air balloon
- ❏ feed the birds

LIFE IS TOO SHORT . . .

Not to:

❏ send a valentine

❏ smile at a baby

❏ mend fences

❏ be cool

❏ make believe

LIFE IS TOO SHORT . . .

❑ to go through the lost and found
❑ to time the pizza delivery man
❑ to use hairpins
❑ to teach an old dog new tricks
❑ to meddle

LIFE IS TOO SHORT . . .

❏ to find out why a shipment goes by car and cargo goes by ship
❏ to figure out how long a short circuit is
❏ to play tennis with dead balls
❏ to paint a picket fence
❏ to name your cat anything but Kitty

Life Is Too Short . . .

Not to:

- ❏ change your mind
- ❏ change your slipcovers
- ❏ change your age

LIFE IS TOO SHORT . . .

Not to:

- ❏ raise hell
- ❏ raise the roof
- ❏ raise your consciousness

Life Is Too Short . . .

❏ to touch your toes when you're eight
   months pregnant
❏ to touch your toes when you're over sixty
❏ to touch your toes after you've eaten dessert
❏ to touch your toes, period

LIFE IS TOO SHORT . . .

❏ to iron a white linen shirt
❏ to figure out where it went wrong
❏ to redo your Rolodex
❏ to look before you leap
❏ to dust every slat on a mini-blind

LIFE IS TOO SHORT . . .

❑ to pick lint off anything
❑ to write thank-you notes on your
  honeymoon
❑ to gild a lily
❑ to take bagpipe lessons
❑ to reinvent the wheel

LIFE IS TOO SHORT . . .

❑ to worry if extraterrestrials are living among us
❑ to join a soap opera discussion group
❑ to search for subliminal messages on TV
❑ to take your pet to psychiatric counseling
❑ to suffer from ennui

LIFE IS TOO SHORT . . .

Not to:

- ❑ sleep naked
- ❑ wear red toenail polish in the summer
- ❑ read the comics
- ❑ let go
- ❑ cuddle

LIFE IS TOO SHORT . . .

Not to:

- ❑ eat the cookie dough
- ❑ carry jumper cables in your car
- ❑ ask for help
- ❑ surprise someone with a smile
- ❑ phone home

LIFE IS TOO SHORT . . .

❏ to memorize birthdays and anniversaries
❏ to invent your own low-calorie dairy dessert
❏ to polish your tires
❏ to read junk mail
❏ to cut your own hair

LIFE IS TOO SHORT . . .

❏ to be room mother
❏ to cut off the crusts
❏ to find the gas gauge on "E"
❏ to be sick on a snow day
❏ to please everyone

LIFE IS TOO SHORT . . .

❑ to iron wrapping paper
❑ to alphabetize your coupons
❑ to worry about asteroid impact
❑ to wait for the video to come out

LIFE IS TOO SHORT . . .

❏ to fawn, grovel, or worry
❏ to wear a girdle
❏ to find a needle in a haystack
❏ to make your own wine

LIFE IS TOO SHORT . . .

❏ to wait for your shoes–or your jeans–to
  stretch
❏ to forget election promises
❏ to swim with sharks
❏ to hate your ex
❏ to get sand in your bathing suit

LIFE IS TOO SHORT . . .

❏ to study hieroglyphics
❏ to count on savings and loans
❏ to argue with a teenager
❏ to wonder what the founding fathers would
  have done about it
❏ to put up with a Type A personality

LIFE IS TOO SHORT . . .

Not to:

- ❏ use real maple syrup
- ❏ try a new toothpaste
- ❏ believe in wrinkle cream
- ❏ know how to say no

LIFE IS TOO SHORT . . .

Not to:

- ❏ swim with dolphins
- ❏ dance all night
- ❏ take a shortcut
- ❏ ask directions

LIFE IS TOO SHORT . . .

Not to:

❏ back up your hard drive
❏ read to the kids
❏ build a sand castle
❏ ask for what you want
❏ love rainy days, too

LIFE IS TOO SHORT . . .

❏ to lose your nerve
         your serve
         or your verve

LIFE IS TOO SHORT . . .

❑ to read about it—because

LIFE IS TOO SHORT!

ABOUT THE AUTHORS

HELEN BLAND has been known to gambol and cavort on the first day of spring.

PATTI FALZARANO doesn't dust the top of her refrigerator unless expecting tall visitors, and she could never give up chocolate.

BO NILES refuses to sort socks.

MARY SEARS wears leopard spike heels to Republican rallies.